# The Beauty of

# BERMUDA

PREVIOUS BOOKS BY SCOTT STALLARD
*BERMUDA*
*BERMUDA II*
*BERMUDA Aerial Views*

Photographs © Scott Stallard, St George, Bermuda
Introduction © Peter Benchley, Princeton, New Jersey
Designed by Roger Boulton, Toronto
Printed and bound in China by Book Art Inc, Toronto
ISBN 0-920831-14-1

# *The Beauty of*

# BERMUDA

## SCOTT STALLARD

## with an Introduction by
## PETER BENCHLEY

### OAKWELL
### BOULTON

This book is dedicated to my mother
MARGARET EMILY STALLARD
1930–1992

and to the arrival of my son
KADE CONNOR STALLARD
15 JULY 1993

So the fullness of things is always being renewed,
As the generations change,
And, like runners, they pass on the torch of life.
Lucretius

# AUTHOR'S PREFACE

Before I say anything about this book, or indeed anything more at all, I wish to thank my father Sidney Stallard and my friend Jonathan Wainwright for their unfailing support.

I don't spend much time thinking about why I take photographs, but I do spend a lot of time doing it! Too impatient to paint, I gravitated towards producing images on film, tens of thousands of them eventually. I suppose it has become a compulsion, since I don't seem able to take a trip without cameras and a stockphoto list from Image Bank.

Happily this compulsion translated into good fortune some years ago when my publisher Roger Boulton paid me the biggest compliment by asking if his company could publish my pictures of Bermuda in a purely photographic book. Now, four books and 35,000 copies later, I think I finally got the exposure down!

As the first three books will never be reprinted again, having already gone through two editions each, we decided to publish this compilation, presenting my favourite images of Bermuda by sea, by land and by air, with a select few new shots to round it all out.

There is an advantage to this. Books in colour are expensive, because it costs so much to make the printing film. Much of that cost has already been covered and we can now present this new, comprehensive book at a price affordable to a great many more people than before.

When I was at boarding school in England I always tried to find pictures to show my friends where I lived. I was so proud of my little island out in the middle of the ocean. It has taken me some time, but now I am content that I can offer my vision of this island, so that some other schoolchild may show it to friends, or so that a visitor may take it home, as a reminder of where to return.

Photography is a relatively young medium for recording aspects of life. With its ability to produce a near perfect mirror image as well as the rainbow of effects to enhance our personal interpretation, the photograph continues to dominate our lives and to influence our world view.

One photograph of Front Street in early 1900 can show us enough information to fill a written book. What a joy it would be if it were possible to see aerial shots of the island in 1609. But imagine people four hundred years on from now, if they could see the pictures in this book. What would they think? What would they say? Probably just like us:

"Now those were the days!"

SCOTT STALLARD
St George, Bermuda

# INTRODUCTION
## by Peter Benchley

Nearly a quarter of a century ago, I made a snap decision that seemed of little consequence at the time, but that, as fate would have it, changed my and my family's lives forever.

Back then, I was struggling to make a living as a freelance writer. I would scribble about anything for anyone—movie reviews, celebrity interviews, travel pieces—sometimes for fees that barely put gruel on the table or shoes on the children.

A magazine for which I had done a couple of articles offered me a choice of two assignments: I could journey halfway around the world to the Coral Sea and dive with poisonous sea snakes, or I could fly two hours from New York and do a story on Bermuda.

The decision took less than ten seconds. I chose Bermuda, and for an entire glorious month I lived here, scouring the archipelago (Bermuda is not one single island, but more than 100, connected by bridges) from one end to the other, diving in its gin-clear waters, meeting its hospitable and amiable people, learning its enthralling history.

When the research was done, I went home and wrote the article. The magazine accepted it, and paid me. Normally, that would have been the end of the story.

What I couldn't know at the time, however, was that for me the story of Bermuda would never be over. I had become thoroughly captivated by the islands Shakespeare referred to in *The Tempest* as the "still-vex'd Bermoothes." I would come back time and again, year after year, in every season and all weather. I would write two novels about the islands, and would make one feature film ("The Deep") and countless television shows here. My children would learn to dive here, under the tutelage of the prodigious Teddy Tucker, one of the truly great figures in the world of the sea.

What vexed Bermuda in 1612, and vexes it still on occasion, is also its friend and provider: the sea. To quote from myself in that article written long ago, "The Bermudians' affair with the sea has been going on for nearly four centuries. It has been a stormy relationship. The first men to set foot on Bermuda were shipwrecked sailors, though no one is sure when that happened. Officially the islands were discovered sometime before 1515 by the Spaniard Juan de Bermùdez, whose name they bear. The English were the first to settle (again, by shipwreck) in 1609; by then one castaway had taken the extraordinary trouble to carve initials resembling FT, a cross, and the date 1543 in a rock on the south shore."

The entire history of Bermuda can be documented by the hundreds of shipwrecks that lie in the coral reefs that ring the islands. There are sixteenth-century Spanish galleons, seventeenth-century English traders, eighteenth-century tartans, nineteenth-century warships and blockade-runners (from the years of the American Civil War), and twentieth-century steamers.

But Bermuda's history is also visible in its houses, its fortresses, its gardens, its boats and its people, who are of widely varied ancestries. Many are of English stock, of course, for the islands comprise Britain's oldest remaining colony, but there are also descendants of Portuguese sailors, African slaves, immigrants from Europe and Asia, and even Mohican Indians, who were sent from New York to Bermuda as slaves in the seventeenth century.

The lures of Bermuda are legion. Because it is kissed by the Gulf Stream, it enjoys weather uncharacteristically balmy, considering its northern latitude. Never has the temperature dipped below the high 30s, and never has there been a year without at least 340 days of at least some sunshine. Oleander, hibiscus, poinciana, poinsettia, and palm and casuarina trees grow in profusion. A visitor can pluck an orange, a lime or a banana from a tree overhanging a road. Golf, tennis and sailing are enjoyed year round, and even in the depths of winter the water is warm enough for a brisk (if bracing) swim.

No wonder, then, that the islands have become a mecca for some half a million visitors a year. As Mark Twain wrote to a friend more than eighty years ago, "You go to heaven if you want to—I'd druther stay here."

Photographing Bermuda would seem to be easy, but it isn't. Bright colors, pastels, stark contrast and high sunlight can lead the unwary enthusiast into the trap of banality and cliché.

Scott Stallard knows this, and much more; he has an artist's eye and the fine skills of an expert craftsman, and in my judgment in this book he has captured the essence of Bermuda with a stunning blend of subtlety, nuance and vivid brilliance.

Describing photographs is a thankless task; pictures are meant to be looked at, not talked about. As you leaf through *The Beauty of Bermuda*, you'll form your own impressions, which will mean much more to you than could any words of mine.

But I can give you one personal example of why I have for years admired Scott's work. In 1991, I needed a jacket portrait for a novel. As background, I should say that I am notoriously hard to photograph; I usually end up looking surly, sullen, sleepy-eyed or just plain dopey. So, Scott's task was to perform a kind of alchemy, turning a surly (or sullen or sleepy-eyed or dopey) middle-aged writer into a figure attractive enough to grace the back of a book.

He did it, and I signed a print of the picture for him with the following inscription: "For Scott Stallard, magician with a camera."

Bermuda doesn't need an alchemist; its wonders are already here for anyone to experience. But to convey them as splendidly as Scott has done does require a kind of magic.

Read this book, and I'm sure you'll agree.

 PETER BENCHLEY has written eight novels, including *Jaws, The Deep, Beast* and *White Shark*. So far three of them have become movies. He has also written, narrated and appeared in more than a score of television documentaries about the ocean. He has been diving since the early '60s. He was born in New York, graduated from Harvard and lives in Princeton. He is married and has three children. He has been to Bermuda more times than he could possibly count.

*1* Exploring the islands in Elys Harbour, Somerset

2 Looking into Bermuda

3 Coral Beach bending to join Elbow Beach, South Shore, Paget

*4* Burnaby Street meets Front Street, City of Hamilton

5 Red oleander sets off the crisp white brilliance of 'Come Aboard',
 a garden cottage on the harbour, St George

6 Surf's up

7 Relics from days gone by

8 The gardens of the Bermuda Perfumery

*9* The town of St George and its harbour

10 A lizard suns itself on a night-blooming cereus

11 Sunset, Flatt's Inlet

*12* Horseshoe Beach, Southampton

*13* Replica of the *Deliverance* on Ordnance Island, St George

14 Homes along the beautiful Tucker's Town peninsula

15 Under the beach umbrella, Windsor Beach, Tucker's Town

*16* Carly

*17* Sunrise on Elys Harbour

*18* The beach at 'Blue Flag', Mangrove Bay, Somerset

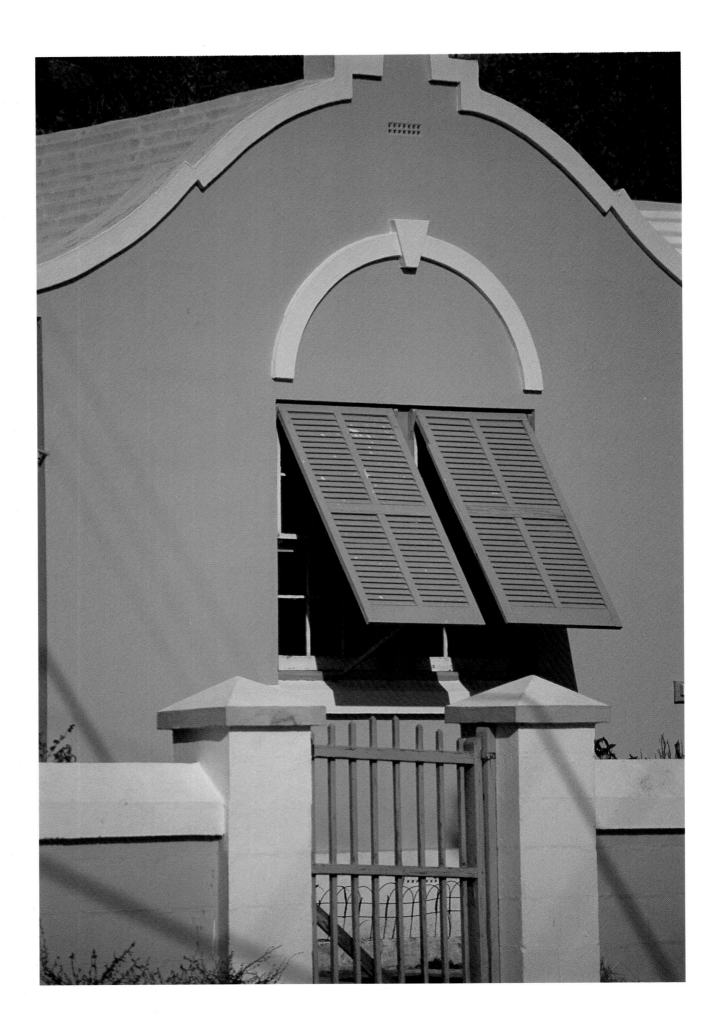

*19* A roadside cottage in Mullet Bay, St George; pink is a popular
colour for houses in Bermuda

*20* Bathers frolic in the surf of Horseshoe Bay

*21* A morning at the aquarium for Glimmerview Nursery School

*22* Trail horses cross the sands of Horseshoe Beach

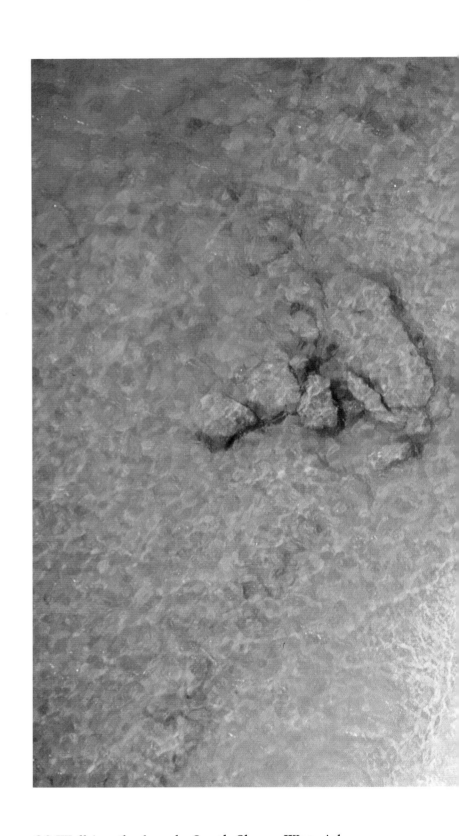

*23* Walking the beach, South Shore, Warwick

*24* Male bluebird

*25* 'Baitbox', Mullet Bay, St George

26 Early light on the verandah

27 A fisherman cuts through the early morning calm,
   in search of bait, Ferry Reach, St George

28 Fitted dinghies, 'Elizabeth', 'Challenger', 'Victory',
   'Bloodhound', 'Contest' and 'Echo'

29 Curried goat and a Pepsi to go!

*30* Cricket match in progress, Wellington Oval, St George

*31* Clean bowled! Cup Match action

*32* Rock formations, South Shore beaches, Warwick

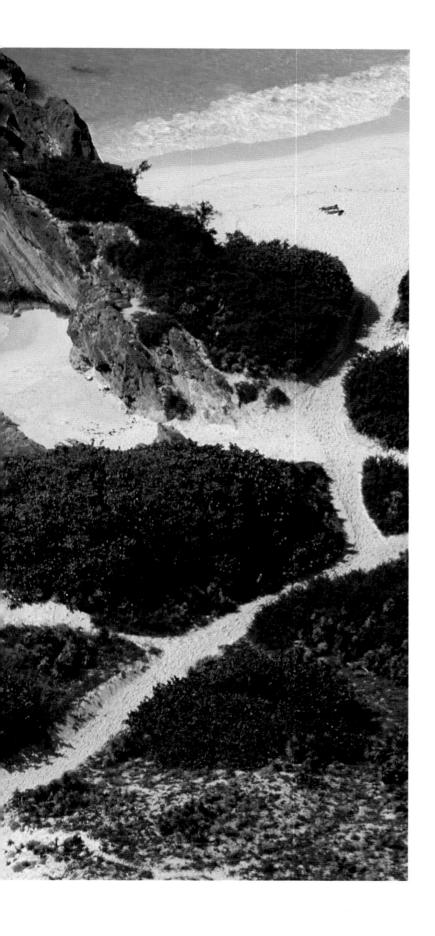

*33* 'Simon's Cottage', High Point, Southampton

*34* An old rough cedar gate, Bailey's Bay

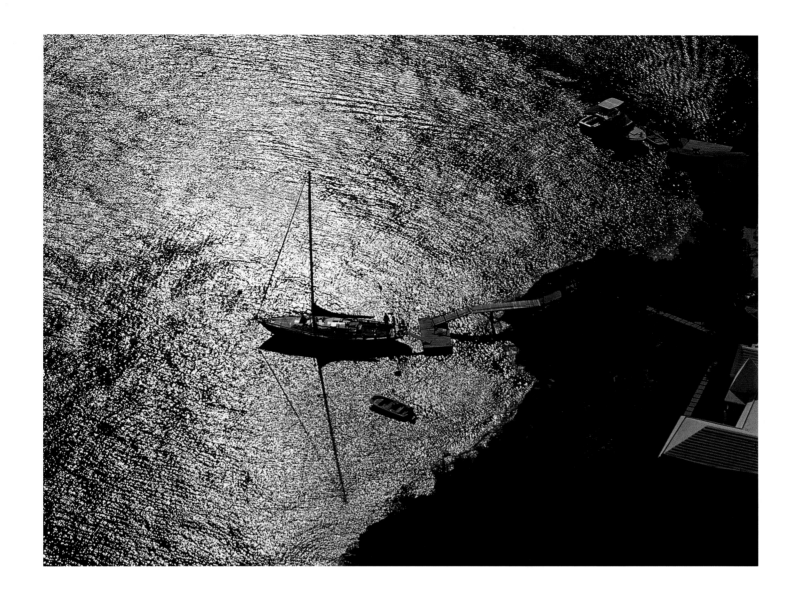

*35* Limestone quarry, Harrington Sound

*36* Yacht at Hinson's Island, stocking up for its voyage north

*37 (overleaf)* Little girl enjoying the annual Cup Match festivities,
    at St George, on the first day of August

*38 (overleaf)* Lone windsurfer sails through the sparkling sea off Sandys

39 Honeybee in search of nectar from a trumpet honeysuckle

40 Sunset hues at Ferry Reach, St George

*41* Fort St Catherine, landing place of Bermuda's first shipwre

d inhabitants

*42* Bay grape and West Indian almond leaves in early September

*43* Working the fields, 'Locust Hall', Devonshire

44 Old bell tower, Sandys

45 The longtail heralds the approach of summer

46 Saltus boys in winter uniform, Saltus Cavendish

47 Coming to nursery school on St Valentine's Day

*48* 'Celtic Green', overlooking Mid-Ocean Golf Course

*49* Mid-Ocean Beach, looking east toward Natural Arches, Tucker's Town

*50* 'Beach Cove', South Shore, Smiths

*51* A proud father greets his daughter on her wedding day

*52* The magnificent Bermuda Easter Lily

53 'Cymru', along Castle Harbour, Tucker's Town

54 A 'push-out blind' at Bridge House, Somerset

*55* Jobson's Cove and horses on the trail, South Shore, Warwick

*56* Horse and buggy on Lighthouse Hill, Southampton

57 Bermuda cherries ripening to red

58 The north roundabout, Foot of the Lane, Paget

*59* A deserted island, Elys Harbour, Sandys

*60* St Peter's Church, St George, oldest Anglican church still in use in the western hemisphere; built in 1612

*61* Local painter at work

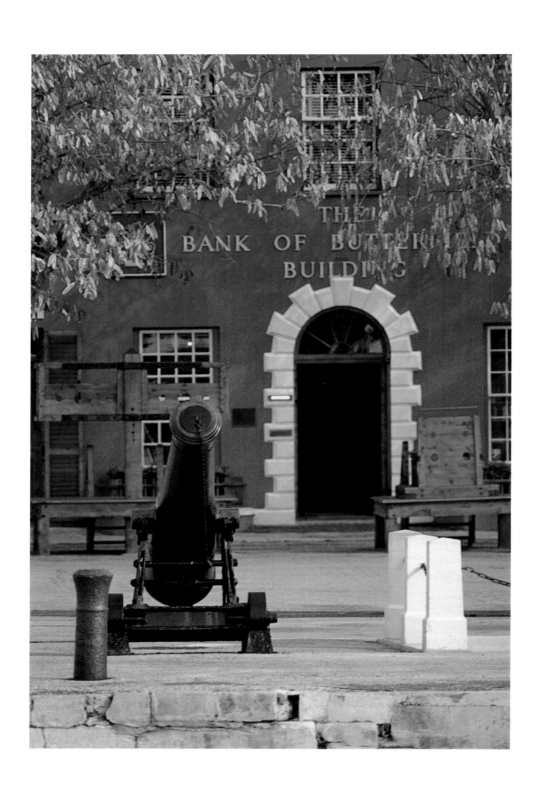

62 The Bank of N.T.Butterfield, with replicas of the stocks and pillory
in front, St George

63 Members of the Bermuda Parliament, in top hats and tails, leaving the
Sessions House on the occasion of the opening of Parliament

64 Chimney design by Tom Watlington in the traditional style and
   method of building

65 A Bermuda roof gets a new coat of whitewash

66 'The Clearing', Tucker's Town

67 Sky, sandstone, soil, sand and sea

68 View to the southeast over Southampton and Riddell's Bay,

wick

69 'The Pampas', shoreline, South Shore, Smiths

70 'Palm Grove', Gibbon's Gardens, Devonshire

*71* The Easter lily field at the Perfume Factory

*72* St George Golf Course, Wellington Oval and Ferry Reach

*73* 'Durham', Old Slip Lane, overlooking Hamilton Harbour

*74* Ploughing potatoes

75 Walter Thompson, a gentleman of St George, with his friend Tiki

76 An old birdhouse sits atop a dead cedar, surrounded by bougainvillea

77 Frick's Point, Tucker's Town

78 Yellow double hibiscus

79 Pawpaw tree, also known as Papaya

*80* Knapton Hill is reflected in Harrington Sound

*81* Views from Trimingham Hill across to the City of Hamilton

*82* Snorkelers enjoying the South Shore in Southampton

*83* A tranquil lane in Somerset, shaded by cedars and Spanish moss

84 A fisherman with bait-nets lies off Boaz Island, Sandys

85 Castle Island and Fort, with Charles Island beyond

*86* Boiler reefs, South Shore

*87* Trunk Island, Harrington Sound

*88* 'Wreck House', Wreck Hill Estate, Sandys

89 Fishing nets drying in Flatts

90 The 'Map of Bermuda' pond, Gibbon's Gardens, Devonshire

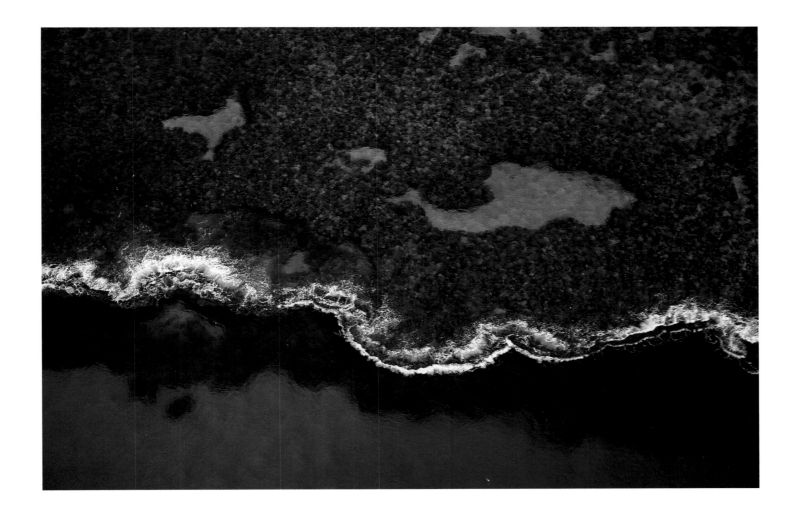

*91* Looking east along South Shore, toward Mid Ocean Beach

*92* South Shore reefline

*93* War veterans on Remembrance Day

*94* St Mark's Church, Smith's Parish

95 Long House, Water Street, St George

96 The home of Joseph Stockdale, who brought the first printing press
to Bermuda in 1783 and founded the *Bermuda Gazette*

*97* The St George Club time-share cottages, overlooking St George Harbour and golf course

*98* Antique buttery roof

*99* Classic design of gable end and rooftops

*100* The unfinished church, Church Folly Lane, St George

*101* Fishing boat and nets, Flatts Village, Smiths

*102* The Bierman Estate, Ferry Reach, St George

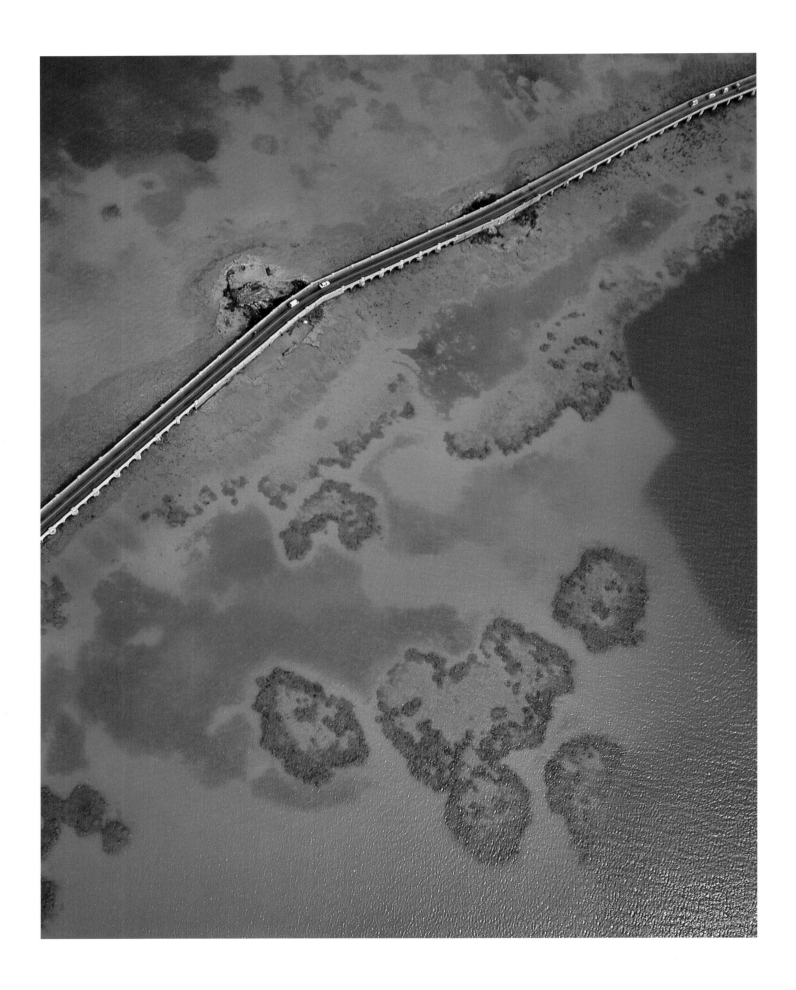

*103* The Causeway perched atop a reef

*104* Shallow sandy waters of Tucker's Town Bay

*105* The Old Rectory behind St Peter's Church, St George

*106* Yachts leaving St George, BOCA Race

*107* 'Sandymount' and Bailey's Bay, looking southward

*108* House signs framed in hibiscus

*109* Immaculate gardens of an island home

*110* Bait fisherman looking for fry, Wreck Bay, Sandys

*111* Little abandoned cottage, Grace Island

*112* 'Dockyard', Ireland Island

*113* Approaching Bermuda from the east

*114* Approaching Bermuda from the northwest at 30,000 feet

*115* Sunset over Great Sound, from the Waterlot Inn, Southampton

*116* Fishermen, Flatts Inlet

*117* Bermuda tree frog, momentarily silent

# ABOUT THE AUTHOR

SCOTT STALLARD was born and raised in Bermuda. He attended school in Bermuda, England and the United States, graduating with a Bachelor of Science degree from Springfield College, Massachusetts. He worked in the hotel and airline industry, and as an actor and a professional model in New York City, and as an assistant to a film producer and is now a health club owner, but his principal interest was always photography.

Self-taught as a photographer, Scott is now represented worldwide by The Image Bank, the largest stockphoto agency in the world. His award-winning work has been widely featured in such publications as *Time, People, Golf Magazine* and *House Beautiful.*

Scott's first exhibition sold out in a few hours. Since then he has gone on to produce over one thousand prints for collectors of the photographic art. His first three books of Bermuda were so widely acclaimed that he was nominated one of the Two Outstanding Young People of 1990. He has in progress an illustrated portrait of historic St George and a